I0465545

GNU Units Manual

A catalogue record for this book is available from the Hong Kong Public Libraries.

Published in Hong Kong by Samurai Media Limited.

Email: info@samuraimedia.org

ISBN 978-988-8381-52-4

Copyright 1996, 1997, 1999, 2000, 2001, 2002, 2004, 2005, 2007, 2011, 2012, 2013, 2014 Free Software Foundation, Inc.
Permission is granted to copy, distribute and/or modify this document under the terms of the GNU Free Documentation License, Version 1.3 or any later version published by the Free Software Foundation; with no Invariant Sections, with no Front-Cover Texts, and with no Back-Cover Texts. A copy of the license is included in the section entitled GNU Free Documentation License.

Minor modifications for publication Copyright 2015 Samurai Media Limited.

Background Cover Image by https://www.flickr.com/people/webtreatsetc/

Table of Contents

1 Overview of units

The units program converts quantities expressed in various systems of measurement to their equivalents in other systems of measurement. Like many similar programs, it can handle multiplicative scale changes. It can also handle nonlinear conversions such as Fahrenheit to Celsius;[1] see Section 6.1 [Temperature Conversions], page 12. The program can also perform conversions from and to sums of units, such as converting between meters and feet plus inches.

Basic operation is simple: you enter the units that you want to convert *from* and the units that you want to convert *to*. You can use the program interactively with prompts, or you can use it from the command line.

Beyond simple unit conversions, units can be used as a general-purpose scientific calculator that keeps track of units in its calculations. You can form arbitrary complex mathematical expressions of dimensions including sums, products, quotients, powers, and even roots of dimensions. Thus you can ensure accuracy and dimensional consistency when working with long expressions that involve many different units that may combine in complex ways; for an illustration, see Section 5.6 [Complicated Unit Expressions], page 11.

The units are defined in an external data file. You can use the extensive data file that comes with this program, or you can provide your own data file to suit your needs. You can also use your own data file to supplement the standard data file.

You can change the default behavior of units with various options given on the command line. See Chapter 9 [Invoking Units], page 20, for a description of the available options.

2 Interacting with units

To invoke units for interactive use, type *units* at your shell prompt. The program will print something like this:

```
Currency exchange rates from www.timegenie.com on 2014-03-05
2860 units, 109 prefixes, 85 nonlinear units
```

```
You have:
```

At the 'You have:' prompt, type the quantity and units that you are converting *from*. For example, if you want to convert ten meters to feet, type *10 meters*. Next, units will print 'You want:'. You should type the units you want to convert *to*. To convert to feet, you would type *feet*. If the readline library was compiled in then TAB will complete unit names. See Chapter 16 [Readline Support], page 39, for more information about readline. To quit the program under Unix, press CTRL-C or CTRL-D. Under Windows, press CTRL-C or CTRL-Z; with the latter, you may also need to press ENTER.

The result will be displayed in two ways. The first line of output, which is marked with a '*' to indicate multiplication, gives the result of the conversion you have asked for. The second line of output, which is marked with a '/' to indicate division, gives the inverse of the conversion factor. If you convert 10 meters to feet, units will print

---

[1] But Fahrenheit to Celsius is linear, you insist. Not so. A transformation T is linear if $T(x + y) = T(x) + T(y)$ and this fails for $T(x) = ax + b$. This transformation is affine, but not linear.

```
        * 32.808399
        / 0.03048
```

which tells you that 10 meters equals about 32.8 feet. The second number gives the conversion in the opposite direction. In this case, it tells you that 1 foot is equal to about 0.03 dekameters since the dekameter is 10 meters. It also tells you that 1/32.8 is about 0.03.

The units program prints the inverse because sometimes it is a more convenient number. In the example above, for example, the inverse value is an exact conversion: a foot is exactly 0.03048 dekameters. But the number given the other direction is inexact.

If you convert grains to pounds, you will see the following:

```
You have: grains
You want: pounds
        * 0.00014285714
        / 7000
```

From the second line of the output you can immediately see that a grain is equal to a seven thousandth of a pound. This is not so obvious from the first line of the output. If you find the output format confusing, try using the '--verbose' option:

```
You have: grain
You want: aeginamina
        grain = 0.00010416667 aeginamina
        grain = (1 / 9600) aeginamina
```

If you request a conversion between units that measure reciprocal dimensions, then units will display the conversion results with an extra note indicating that reciprocal conversion has been done:

```
You have: 6 ohms
You want: siemens
        reciprocal conversion
        * 0.16666667
        / 6
```

Reciprocal conversion can be suppressed by using the '--strict' option. As usual, use the '--verbose' option to get more comprehensible output:

```
You have: tex
You want: typp
        reciprocal conversion
        1 / tex = 496.05465 typp
        1 / tex = (1 / 0.0020159069) typp

You have: 20 mph
You want: sec/mile
        reciprocal conversion
        1 / 20 mph = 180 sec/mile
        1 / 20 mph = (1 / 0.0055555556) sec/mile
```

If you enter incompatible unit types, the units program will print a message indicating that the units are not conformable and it will display the reduced form for each unit:

```
You have: ergs/hour
You want: fathoms kg^2 / day
conformability error
        2.7777778e-11 kg m^2 / sec^3
        2.1166667e-05 kg^2 m / sec
```

If you only want to find the reduced form or definition of a unit, simply press ENTER at the 'You want:' prompt. Here is an example:

```
You have: jansky
You want:
        Definition: fluxunit = 1e-26 W/m^2 Hz = 1e-26 kg / s^2
```

The output from **units** indicates that the jansky is defined to be equal to a fluxunit which in turn is defined to be a certain combination of watts, meters, and hertz. The fully reduced (and in this case somewhat more cryptic) form appears on the far right.

Some named units are treated as dimensionless in some situations. These units include the radian and steradian. These units will be treated as equal to 1 in units conversions. Power is equal to torque times angular velocity. This conversion can only be performed if the radian is dimensionless.

```
You have: (14 ft lbf) (12 radians/sec)
You want: watts
        * 227.77742
        / 0.0043902509
```

Named dimensionless units are not treated as dimensionless in other contexts. They cannot be used as exponents so for example, 'meter^radian' is not allowed.

If you want a list of options you can type **?** at the 'You want:' prompt. The program will display a list of named units that are conformable with the unit that you entered at the 'You have:' prompt above. Conformable unit *combinations* will not appear on this list.

Typing **help** at either prompt displays a short help message. You can also type **help** followed by a unit name. This will invoke a pager on the units data base at the point where that unit is defined. You can read the definition and comments that may give more details or historical information about the unit. (You can generally quit out of the page by pressing 'q'.)

Typing **search** *text* will display a list of all of the units whose names contain *text* as a substring along with their definitions. This may help in the case where you aren't sure of the right unit name.

3 Using units Non-Interactively

The **units** program can perform units conversions non-interactively from the command line. To do this, type the command, type the original unit expression, and type the new units you want. If a units expression contains non-alphanumeric characters, you may need to protect it from interpretation by the shell using single or double quote characters

If you type

```
units "2 liters" quarts
```

then **units** will print

```
        * 2.1133764
        / 0.47317647
```

and then exit. The output tells you that 2 liters is about 2.1 quarts, or alternatively that a quart is about 0.47 times 2 liters.

If the conversion is successful, then **units** will return success (zero) to the calling environment. If you enter non-conformable units then **units** will print a message giving the reduced form of each unit and it will return failure (nonzero) to the calling environment.

When you invoke **units** with only one argument, it will print out the definition of the specified unit. It will return failure if the unit is not defined and success if the unit is defined.

4 Unit Definitions

The conversion information is read from a units data file that is called '**definitions.units**' and is usually located in the '**/usr/share/units**' directory. If you invoke **units** with the '**-V**' option, it will print the location of this file. The default file includes definitions for all familiar units, abbreviations and metric prefixes. It also includes many obscure or archaic units.

Many constants of nature are defined, including these:

pi	ratio of circumference to diameter
c	speed of light
e	charge on an electron
force	acceleration of gravity
mole	Avogadro's number
water	pressure per unit height of water
Hg	pressure per unit height of mercury
au	astronomical unit
k	Boltzman's constant
mu0	permeability of vacuum
epsilon0	permittivity of vacuum
G	Gravitational constant
mach	speed of sound

The standard data file includes atomic masses for all of the elements and numerous other constants. Also included are the densities of various ingredients used in baking so that '2 cups flour_sifted' can be converted to 'grams'. This is not an exhaustive list. Consult the units data file to see the complete list, or to see the definitions that are used.

The 'pound' is a unit of mass. To get force, multiply by the force conversion unit 'force' or use the shorthand 'lbf'. (Note that 'g' is already taken as the standard abbreviation for the gram.) The unit 'ounce' is also a unit of mass. The fluid ounce is 'fluidounce' or 'floz'. When British capacity units differ from their US counterparts, such as the British Imperial gallon, the unit is defined both ways with 'br' and 'us' prefixes. Your locale settings will determine the value of the unprefixed unit. Currency is prefixed with its country name: 'belgiumfranc', 'britainpound'.

When searching for a unit, if the specified string does not appear exactly as a unit name, then the **units** program will try to remove a trailing 's', 'es'. Next units will replace a trailing 'ies' with 'y'. If that fails, units will check for a prefix. The database includes all of the standard metric prefixes. Only one prefix is permitted per unit, so 'micromicrofarad' will fail. However, prefixes can appear alone with no unit following them, so 'micro*microfarad' will work, as will 'micro microfarad'.

To find out which units and prefixes are available, read the standard units data file, which is extensively annotated.

4.1 English Customary Units

English customary units differ in various ways in different regions. In Britain a complex system of volume measurements featured different gallons for different materials such as a wine gallon and ale gallon that different by twenty percent. This complexity was swept away in 1824 by a reform that created an entirely new gallon, the British Imperial gallon defined as the volume occupied by ten pounds of water. Meanwhile in the USA the gallon is derived from the 1707 Winchester wine gallon, which is 231 cubic inches. These gallons differ by about twenty percent. By default if units runs in the 'en_GB' locale you will get the British volume measures. If it runs in the 'en_US' locale you will get the US volume measures. In other locales the default values are the US definitions. If you wish to force different definitions then set the environment variable UNITS_ENGLISH to either 'US' or 'GB' to set the desired definitions independent of the locale.

Before 1959, the value of a yard (and other units of measure defined in terms of it) differed slightly among English-speaking countries. In 1959, Australia, Canada, New Zealand the United Kingdom, the United States, and South Africa adopted the Canadian value of 1 yard = 0.9144 m (exactly), which was approximately halfway between the values used by the UK and the US; it had the additional advantage of making 1 inch = 2.54 cm (exactly). This new standard was termed the *International Yard*. Australia, Canada, and the UK then defined all customary lengths in terms of the International Yard (Australia did not define the furlong or rod); because many US land surveys were in terms of the pre-1959 units, the US continued to define customary surveyors' units (furlong, chain, rod, and link) in terms of the previous value for the foot, which was termed the *US survey foot*. The US defined a *US survey mile* as 5280 US survey feet, and defined a *statute mile* as a US survey mile. The US values for these units differ from the international values by about 2 ppm.

The units program uses the international values for these units; the US values can be obtained by using either the 'US' or the 'survey' prefix. In either case, the simple familiar relationships among the units are maintained, e.g., 1 'furlong' = 660 'ft', and 1 'USfurlong' = 660 'USft', though the metric equivalents differ slightly between the two cases. The 'US' prefix or the 'survey' prefix can also be used to obtain the US survey mile and the value of the US yard prior to 1959, e.g., 'USmile' or 'surveymile' (but *not* 'USsurveymile'). To get the US value of the statute mile, use either 'USstatutemile' or 'USmile'.

Except for distances that extend over hundreds of miles (such as in the US State Plane Coordinate System), the differences in the miles are usually insignificant:

```
You have: 100 surveymile - 100 mile
You want: inch
        * 12.672025
        / 0.078913984
```

The pre-1959 UK values for these units can be obtained with the prefix 'UK'.

In the US, the acre is officially defined in terms of the US survey foot, but **units** uses a definition based on the international foot. If you want the official US acre use 'USacre' and similarly use 'USacrefoot' for the official US version of that unit. The difference between these units is about 4 parts per million.

5 Unit Expressions

5.1 Operators

You can enter more complicated units by combining units with operations such as multiplication, division, powers, addition, subtraction, and parentheses for grouping. You can use the customary symbols for these operators when **units** is invoked with its default options. Additionally, **units** supports some extensions, including high priority multiplication using a space, and a high priority numerical division operator ('|') that can simplify some expressions.

You multiply units using a space or an asterisk ('*'). The next example shows both forms:

```
You have: arabicfoot * arabictradepound * force
You want: ft lbf
        * 0.7296
        / 1.370614
```

You can divide units using the slash ('/') or with 'per':

```
You have: furlongs per fortnight
You want: m/s
        * 0.00016630986
        / 6012.8727
```

You can use parentheses for grouping:

```
You have: (1/2) kg / (kg/meter)
You want: league
        * 0.00010356166
        / 9656.0833
```

Multiplication using a space has a higher precedence than division using a slash and is evaluated left to right; in effect, the first '/' character marks the beginning of the denominator of a unit expression. This makes it simple to enter a quotient with several terms in the denominator: 'J / mol K'. The '*' and '/' operators have the same precedence, and are evaluated left to right; if you multiply with '*', you must group the terms in the denominator with parentheses: 'J / (mol * K)'.

The higher precedence of the space operator may not always be advantageous. For example, 'm/s s/day' is equivalent to 'm / s s day' and has dimensions of length per time cubed. Similarly, '1/2 meter' refers to a unit of reciprocal length equivalent to 0.5/meter, perhaps not what you would intend if you entered that expression. The get a half meter you would need to use parentheses: '(1/2) meter'. The '*' operator is convenient for multiplying a sequence of quotients. For example, 'm/s * s/day' is equivalent to 'm/day'. Similarly, you could write '1/2 * meter' to get half a meter.

The units program supports another option for numerical fractions: you can indicate division of *numbers* with the vertical bar ('|'), so if you wanted half a meter you could write '1|2 meter'. You cannot use the vertical bar to indicate division of non-numerical units (e.g., 'm|s' results in an error message).

Powers of units can be specified using the '^' character, as shown in the following example, or by simple concatenation of a unit and its exponent: 'cm3' is equivalent to 'cm^3'; if the exponent is more than one digit, the '^' is required. You can also use '**' as an exponent operator.

```
You have: cm^3
You want: gallons
        * 0.00026417205
        / 3785.4118
```

Concatenation only works with a single unit name: if you write '(m/s)2', units will treat it as multiplication by 2. When a unit includes a prefix, exponent operators apply to the combination, so 'centimeter3' gives cubic centimeters. If you separate the prefix from the unit with any multiplication operator (e.g., 'centi meter^3'), the prefix is treated as a separate unit, so the exponent applies only to the unit without the prefix. The second example is equivalent to 'centi * (meter^3)', and gives a hundredth of a cubic meter, not a cubic centimeter. The units program is limited internally to products of 99 units; accordingly, expressions like 'meter^100' or 'joule^34' (represented internally as 'kg^34 m^68 / s^68') will fail.

The '|' operator has the highest precedence, so you can write the square root of two thirds as '2|3^1|2'. The '^' operator has the second highest precedence, and is evaluated right to left, as usual:

```
You have: 5 * 2^3^2
You want:
          Definition: 2560
```

With a dimensionless base unit, any dimensionless exponent is meaningful (e.g., 'pi^exp(2.371)'). Even though angle is sometimes treated as dimensionless, exponents cannot have dimensions of angle:

```
You have: 2^radian
                 ^
```

Exponent not dimensionless

If the base unit is not dimensionless, the exponent must be a rational number p/q, and the dimension of the unit must be a power of q, so 'gallon^2|3' works but 'acre^2|3' fails. An exponent using the slash ('/') operator (e.g., 'acre^(2/3)') is also acceptable; the parentheses are needed because the precedence of '^' is higher than that of '/'. Since units cannot represent dimensions with exponents greater than 99, a fully reduced exponent must have $q < 100$. When raising a non-dimensionless unit to a power, units attempts to convert a decimal exponent to a rational number with $q < 100$. If this is not possible units displays an error message:

```
You have: ft^1.234
Base unit not dimensionless; rational exponent required
```

A decimal exponent must match its rational representation to machine precision, so 'acre^1.5' works but 'gallon^0.666' does not.

5.2 Sums and Differences of Units

You may sometimes want to add values of different units that are outside the SI. You may also wish to use units as a calculator that keeps track of units. Sums of conformable units are written with the '+' character, and differences with the '-' character.

```
You have: 2 hours + 23 minutes + 32 seconds
You want: seconds
        * 8612
        / 0.00011611705

You have: 12 ft + 3 in
You want: cm
        * 373.38
        / 0.0026782366

You have: 2 btu + 450 ft lbf
You want: btu
        * 2.5782804
        / 0.38785542
```

The expressions that are added or subtracted must reduce to identical expressions in primitive units, or an error message will be displayed:

```
You have: 12 printerspoint - 4 heredium
                                        ^
Illegal sum of non-conformable units
```

As usual, the precedence for '+' and '-' is lower than that of the other operators. A fractional quantity such as 2 1/2 cups can be given as '(2+1|2) cups'; the parentheses are necessary because multiplication has higher precedence than addition. If you omit the parentheses, units attempts to add '2' and '1|2 cups', and you get an error message:

```
You have: 2+1|2 cups
               ^
Illegal sum or difference of non-conformable units
```

The expression could also be correctly written as '(2+1/2) cups'. If you write '2 1|2 cups' the space is interpreted as *multiplication* so the result is the same as '1 cup'.

The '+' and '-' characters sometimes appears in exponents like '3.43e+8'. This leads to an ambiguity in an expression like '3e+2 yC'. The unit 'e' is a small unit of charge, so this can be regarded as equivalent to '(3e+2) yC' or '(3 e)+(2 yC)'. This ambiguity is resolved by always interpreting '+' and '-' as part of an exponent if possible.

5.3 Numbers as Units

For units, numbers are just another kind of unit. They can appear as many times as you like and in any order in a unit expression. For example, to find the volume of a box that is 2 ft by 3 ft by 12 ft in steres, you could do the following:

```
You have: 2 ft 3 ft 12 ft
You want: stere
        * 2.038813
        / 0.49048148

You have: $ 5 / yard
You want: cents / inch
        * 13.888889
        / 0.072
```

And the second example shows how the dollar sign in the units conversion can precede the five. Be careful: units will interpret '$5' with no space as equivalent to 'dollar^5'.

5.4 Built-in Functions

Several built-in functions are provided: 'sin', 'cos', 'tan', 'ln', 'log', 'log2', 'exp', 'acos', 'atan' and 'asin'. The 'sin', 'cos', and 'tan' functions require either a dimensionless argument or an argument with dimensions of angle.

```
You have: sin(30 degrees)
You want:
        Definition: 0.5

You have: sin(pi/2)
You want:
        Definition: 1

You have: sin(3 kg)
                ^

Unit not dimensionless
```

The other functions on the list require dimensionless arguments. The inverse trigonometric functions return arguments with dimensions of angle.

If you wish to take roots of units, you may use the 'sqrt' or 'cuberoot' functions. These functions require that the argument have the appropriate root. You can obtain higher roots by using fractional exponents:

```
You have: sqrt(acre)
You want: feet
        * 208.71074
        / 0.0047913202

You have: (400 W/m^2 / stefanboltzmann)^(1/4)
You have:
        Definition: 289.80882 K

You have: cuberoot(hectare)
                ^

Unit not a root
```

5.5 Previous Result

You can insert the result of the previous conversion using the underscore ('_'). It is useful when you want to convert the same input to several different units, for example

```
You have: 2.3 tonrefrigeration
You want: btu/hr
        * 27600
        / 3.6231884e-005
You have: _
You want: kW
        * 8.0887615
        / 0.12362832
```

Suppose you want to do some deep frying that requires an oil depth of 2 inches. You have 1/2 gallon of oil, and want to know the largest-diameter pan that will maintain the required depth. The nonlinear unit 'circlearea' gives the *radius* of the circle (see Section 6.2 [Other Nonlinear Units], page 13, for a more detailed description) in SI units; you want the *diameter* in *inches*:

```
You have: 1|2 gallon / 2 in
You want: circlearea
        0.10890173 m

You have: 2 _
You want: in
        * 8.5749393
        / 0.1166189
```

In most cases, surrounding white space is optional, so the previous example could have used '2_'. If '_' follows a non-numerical unit symbol, however, the space is required:

```
You have: m_
          ^

Parse error
```

When '_' is followed by a digit, the operation is multiplication rather than exponentiation, so that '_2', is equivalent to '_ * 2' rather than '_^2'.

You can use the '_' symbol any number of times; for example,

```
You have: m
You want:
          Definition: 1 m
You have: _ _
You want:
          Definition: 1 m^2
```

Using '_' before a conversion has been performed (e.g., immediately after invocation) generates an error:

```
You have: _
          ^

No previous result; '_' not set
```

Accordingly, '_' serves no purpose when **units** is invoked non-interactively.

If units is invoked with the '--verbose' option (see Chapter 9 [Invoking Units], page 20), the value of '_' is not expanded

```
You have: mile
You want: ft
        mile = 5280 ft
        mile = (1 / 0.00018939394) ft
You have: _
You want: m
        _ = 1609.344 m
        _ = (1 / 0.00062137119) m
```

You can give '_' at the 'You want:' prompt, but it usually is not very useful.

5.6 Complicated Unit Expressions

The units program is especially helpful in ensuring accuracy and dimensional consistency when converting lengthy unit expressions. For example, one form of the Darcy–Weisbach fluid-flow equation is

$$\Delta P = \frac{8}{\pi^2} \rho f L \frac{Q^2}{d^5}$$

where ΔP is the pressure drop, ρ is the mass density, f is the (dimensionless) friction factor, L is the length of the pipe, Q is the volumetric flow rate, and d is the pipe diameter. It might be desired to have the equation in the form

$$\Delta P = A_1 \rho f L \frac{Q^2}{d^5}$$

that accepted the user's normal units; for typical units used in the US, the required conversion could be something like

```
You have: (8/pi^2)(lbm/ft^3)ft(ft^3/s)^2(1/in^5)
You want: psi
        * 43.533969
        / 0.022970568
```

The parentheses allow individual terms in the expression to be entered naturally as they might be read from the formula. Alternatively, the multiplication could be done with the '*' rather than a space; then parentheses are needed only around 'ft^3/s' because of its exponent:

```
You have: 8/pi^2 * lbm/ft^3 * ft * (ft^3/s)^2 /in^5
You want: psi
        * 43.533969
        / 0.022970568
```

Without parentheses, and using spaces for multiplication, the previous conversion would need to be entered as

```
You have: 8 lb ft ft^3 ft^3 / pi^2 ft^3 s^2 in^5
You want: psi
        * 43.533969
        / 0.022970568
```

5.7 Backwards Compatibility: '*' and '-'

The original **units** assigned multiplication a higher precedence than division using the slash. This differs from the usual precedence rules, which give multiplication and division equal precedence, and can be confusing for people who think of units as a calculator.

The star operator ('*') included in this **units** program has, by default, the same precedence as division, and hence follows the usual precedence rules. For backwards compatibility you can invoke **units** with the '--oldstar' option. Then '*' has a higher precedence than division, and the same precedence as multiplication using the space.

Historically, the hyphen ('-') has been used in technical publications to indicate products of units, and the original **units** program treated it as a multiplication operator. Because **units** provides several other ways to obtain unit products, and because '-' is a subtraction operator in general algebraic expressions, **units** treats the binary '-' as a subtraction operator by default. For backwards compatibility use the '--product' option, which causes **units** to treat the binary '-' operator as a product operator. When '-' is a multiplication operator it has the same precedence as multiplication with a space, giving it a higher precedence than division.

When '-' is used as a unary operator it negates its operand. Regardless of the **units** options, if '-' appears after '(' or after '+' then it will act as a negation operator. So you can always compute 20 degrees minus 12 minutes by entering '20 degrees + -12 arcmin'. You must use this construction when you define new units because you cannot know what options will be in force when your definition is processed.

6 Nonlinear Unit Conversions

Nonlinear units are represented using functional notation. They make possible nonlinear unit conversions such as temperature.

6.1 Temperature Conversions

Conversions between temperatures are different from linear conversions between temperature *increments*—see the example below. The absolute temperature conversions are handled by units starting with 'temp', and you must use functional notation. The temperature-increment conversions are done using units starting with 'deg' and they do not require functional notation.

```
You have: tempF(45)
You want: tempC
        7.2222222

You have: 45 degF
You want: degC
        * 25
        / 0.04
```

Think of 'tempF(x)' not as a function but as a notation that indicates that x should have units of 'tempF' attached to it. See Section 10.3 [Defining Nonlinear Units], page 27. The first conversion shows that if it's 45 degrees Fahrenheit outside, it's 7.2 degrees Celsius. The second conversion indicates that a change of 45 degrees Fahrenheit corresponds to a change of 25 degrees Celsius. The conversion from 'tempF(x)' is to absolute temperature, so that

```
You have: tempF(45)
You want: degR
        * 504.67
        / 0.0019814929
```

gives the same result as

```
You have: tempF(45)
You want: tempR
        * 504.67
        / 0.0019814929
```

But if you convert 'tempF(x)' to 'degC', the output is probably not what you expect:

```
You have: tempF(45)
You want: degC
        * 280.37222
        / 0.0035666871
```

The result is the temperature in K, because 'degC' is defined as 'K', the Kelvin. For consistent results, use the 'tempX' units when converting to a temperature rather than converting a temperature increment.

The 'tempC()' and 'tempF()' definitions are limited to positive absolute temperatures, and giving a value that would result in a negative absolute temperature generates an error message:

```
You have: tempC(-275)
                    ^
Argument of function outside domain
                    ^
```

6.2 Other Nonlinear Units

Some other examples of nonlinear units are numerous different ring sizes and wire gauges, the grit sizes used for abrasives, the decibel scale, shoe size, scales for the density of sugar (e.g., baume). The standard data file also supplies units for computing the area of a circle and the volume of a sphere. See the standard units data file for more details. Wire gauges with multiple zeroes are signified using negative numbers where two zeroes is '-1'. Alternatively, you can use the synonyms 'g00', 'g000', and so on that are defined in the standard units data file.

```
You have: wiregauge(11)
You want: inches
        * 0.090742002
        / 11.020255

You have: brwiregauge(g00)
You want: inches
        * 0.348
        / 2.8735632

You have: 1 mm
You want: wiregauge
        18.201919

You have: grit_P(600)
You want: grit_ansicoated
        342.76923
```

The last example shows the conversion from P graded sand paper, which is the European standard and may be marked "P600" on the back, to the USA standard.

You can compute the area of a circle using the nonlinear unit, 'circlearea'. You can also do this using the circularinch or circleinch. The next example shows two ways to compute the area of a circle with a five inch radius and one way to compute the volume of a sphere with a radius of one meter.

```
You have: circlearea(5 in)
You want: in2
        * 78.539816
        / 0.012732395

You have: 10^2 circleinch
You want: in2
        * 78.539816
        / 0.012732395

You have: spherevol(meter)
You want: ft3
        * 147.92573
        / 0.0067601492
```

The inverse of a nonlinear conversion is indicated by prefixing a tilde ('~') to the nonlinear unit name:

```
You have: ~wiregauge(0.090742002 inches)
You want:
        Definition: 11
```

You can give a nonlinear unit definition without an argument or parentheses, and press ENTER at the 'You want:' prompt to get the definition of a nonlinear unit; if the definition is not valid for all real numbers, the range of validity is also given. If the definition requires specific units this information is also displayed:

```
You have: tempC
        Definition: tempC(x) = x K + stdtemp
                    defined for x >= -273.15
You have: ~tempC
        Definition: ~tempC(tempC) = (tempC +(-stdtemp))/K
                    defined for tempC >= 0 K
You have: circlearea
        Definition: circlearea(r) = pi r^2
                    r has units m
```

To see the definition of the inverse use the '~' notation. In this case the parameter in the functional definition will usually be the name of the unit. Note that the inverse for 'tempC' shows that it requires units of 'K' in the specification of the allowed range of values. Nonlinear unit conversions are described in more detail in Section 10.3 [Defining Nonlinear Units], page 27.

7 Unit Lists: Conversion to Sums of Units

Outside of the SI, it is sometimes desirable to convert a single unit to a sum of units—for example, feet to feet plus inches. The conversion *from* sums of units was described in Section 5.2 [Sums and Differences of Units], page 8, and is a simple matter of adding the units with the '+' sign:

```
You have: 12 ft + 3 in + 3|8 in
You want: ft
        * 12.28125
        / 0.081424936
```

Although you can similarly write a sum of units to convert *to*, the result will not be the conversion to the units in the sum, but rather the conversion to the particular sum that you have entered:

```
You have: 12.28125 ft
You want: ft + in + 1|8 in
        * 11.228571
        / 0.089058524
```

The unit expression given at the 'You want:' prompt is equivalent to asking for conversion to multiples of '1 ft + 1 in + 1|8 in', which is 1.09375 ft, so the conversion in the previous example is equivalent to

```
You have: 12.28125 ft
You want: 1.09375 ft
        * 11.228571
        / 0.089058524
```

In converting to a sum of units like miles, feet and inches, you typically want the largest integral value for the first unit, followed by the largest integral value for the next, and the remainder converted to the last unit. You can do this conversion easily with units using a special syntax for lists of units. You must list the desired units in order from largest to smallest, separated by the semicolon (';') character:

```
You have: 12.28125 ft
You want: ft;in;1|8 in
          12 ft + 3 in + 3|8 in
```

The conversion always gives integer coefficients on the units in the list, except possibly the last unit when the conversion is not exact:

```
You have: 12.28126 ft
You want: ft;in;1|8 in
          12 ft + 3 in + 3.00096 * 1|8 in
```

The order in which you list the units is important:

```
You have: 3 kg
You want: oz;lb
          105 oz + 0.051367866 lb
```

```
You have: 3 kg
You want: lb;oz
          6 lb + 9.8218858 oz
```

Listing ounces before pounds produces a technically correct result, but not a very useful one. You must list the units in descending order of size in order to get the most useful result.

Ending a unit list with the separator ';' has the same effect as repeating the last unit on the list, so 'ft;in;1|8 in;' is equivalent to 'ft;in;1|8 in;1|8 in'. With the example above, this gives

```
You have: 12.28126 ft
You want: ft;in;1|8 in;
          12 ft + 3 in + 3|8 in + 0.00096 * 1|8 in
```

in effect separating the integer and fractional parts of the coefficient for the last unit. If you instead prefer to round the last coefficient to an integer you can do this with the '--round' ('-r') option. With the previous example, the result is

```
You have: 12.28126 ft
You want: ft;in;1|8 in
          12 ft + 3 in + 3|8 in (rounded down to nearest 1|8 in)
```

When you use the '-r' option, repeating the last unit on the list has no effect (e.g., 'ft;in;1|8 in;1|8 in' is equivalent to 'ft;in;1|8 in'), and hence neither does ending a list with a ';'. With a single unit and the '-r' option, a terminal ';' *does* have an effect: it causes **units** to treat the single unit as a list and produce a rounded value for the single unit. Without the extra ';', the '-r' option has no effect on single unit conversions. This example shows the output using the '-r' option:

```
You have: 12.28126 ft
You want: in
          * 147.37512
          / 0.0067854058
```

```
You have: 12.28126 ft
You want: in;
          147 in (rounded down to nearest in)
```

Each unit that appears in the list must be conformable with the first unit on the list, and of course the listed units must also be conformable with the unit that you enter at the 'You have:' prompt.

```
You have: meter
You want: ft;kg
          ^

conformability error
        ft = 0.3048 m
        kg = 1 kg

You have: meter
You want: lb;oz
conformability error
        1 m
        0.45359237 kg
```

In the first case, units reports the disagreement between units appearing on the list. In the second case, units reports disagreement between the unit you entered and the desired conversion. This conformability error is based on the first unit on the unit list.

Other common candidates for conversion to sums of units are angles and time:

```
You have: 23.437754 deg
You want; deg;arcmin;arcsec
    23 deg + 26 arcmin + 15.9144 arcsec

You have: 7.2319 hr
You want: hr;min;sec
    7 hr + 13 min + 54.84 sec
```

In North America, recipes for cooking typically measure ingredients by volume, and use units that are not always convenient multiples of each other. Suppose that you have a recipe for 6 and you wish to make a portion for 1. If the recipe calls for 2 1/2 cups of an ingredient, you might wish to know the measurements in terms of measuring devices you have available, you could use units and enter

```
You have: (2+1|2) cup / 6
You want: cup;1|2 cup;1|3 cup;1|4 cup;tbsp;tsp;1|2 tsp;1|4 tsp
        1|3 cup + 1 tbsp + 1 tsp
```

By default, if a unit in a list begins with fraction of the form $1|x$ and its multiplier is an integer, the fraction is given as the product of the multiplier and the numerator; for example,

```
You have: 12.28125 ft
You want: ft;in;1|8 in;
        12 ft + 3 in + 3 8 in
```

In many cases, such as the example above, this is what is wanted, but sometimes it is not. For example, a cooking recipe for 6 might call for 5 1/4 cup of an ingredient, but you want a portion for 2, and your 1-cup measure is not available; you might try

```
You have: (5+1|4) cup / 3
You want: 1|2 cup;1|3 cup;1|4 cup
        3|2 cup + 1|4 cup
```

This result might be fine for a baker who has a 1 1/2-cup measure (and recognizes the equivalence), but it may not be as useful to someone with more limited set of measures, who does want to do additional calculations, and only wants to know "How many 1/2-cup measures to I need to add?" After all, that's what was actually asked. With the '--show-factor' option, the factor will not be combined with a unity numerator, so that you get

```
You have: (5+1|4) cup / 3
You want: 1|2 cup;1|3 cup;1|4 cup
        3 * 1|2 cup + 1|4 cup
```

A user-specified fractional unit with a numerator other than 1 is never overridden, however— if a unit list specifies '3|4 cup;1|2 cup', a result equivalent to 1 1/2 cups will always be shown as '2 * 3|4 cup' whether or not the '--show-factor' option is given.

Some applications for unit lists may be less obvious. Suppose that you have a postal scale and wish to ensure that it's accurate at 1 oz, but have only metric calibration weights. You might try

```
You have: 1 oz
You want: 100 g;50 g; 20 g;10 g;5 g;2 g;1 g;
        20 g + 5 g + 2 g + 1 g + 0.34952312 * 1 g
```

You might then place one each of the 20 g, 5 g, 2 g, and 1 g weights on the scale and hope that it indicates close to

```
You have: 20 g + 5 g + 2 g + 1 g
You want: oz;
        0.98767093 oz
```

Appending ';' to 'oz' forces a one-line display that includes the unit; here the integer part of the result is zero, so it is not displayed.

A unit list such as

```
cup;1|2 cup;1|3 cup;1|4 cup;tbsp;tsp;1|2 tsp;1|4 tsp
```

can be tedious to enter. The **units** program provides shorthand names for some common combinations:

hms	hours, minutes, seconds
dms	angle: degrees, minutes, seconds
time	years, days, hours, minutes and seconds
usvol	US cooking volume: cups and smaller

Using these shorthands, or *unit list aliases*, you can do the following conversions:

```
You have: anomalisticyear
You want: time
        1 year + 25 min + 3.4653216 sec
You have: 1|6 cup
You want: usvol
        2 tbsp + 2 tsp
```

You cannot combine a unit list alias with other units: it must appear alone at the 'You want:' prompt.

You can display the definition of a unit list alias by entering it at the 'You have:' prompt:

```
You have: dms
        Definition: unit list, deg;arcmin;arcsec
```

When you specify compact output with '--compact', '--terse' or '-t' and perform conversion to a unit list, units lists the conversion factors for each unit in the list, separated by semicolons.

```
You have: year
You want: day;min;sec
365;348;45.974673
```

Unlike the case of regular output, zeros *are* included in this output list:

```
You have: liter
You want: cup;1|2 cup;1|4 cup;tbsp
4;0;0;3.6280454
```

8 Logging Calculations

The '--log' option allows you to save the results of calculations in a file; this can be useful if you need a permanent record of your work. For example, the fluid-flow conversion in Section 5.6 [Complicated Unit Expressions], page 11, is lengthy, and if you were to use it in designing a piping system, you might want a record of it for the project file. If the interactive session

```
You have: (8/pi^2)(lbm/ft^3)ft(ft^3/s)^2(1/in^5)
You want: psi
        * 43.533969
        / 0.022970568
```

were logged, the log file would contain

```
From: (8/pi^2)(lbm/ft^3)ft(ft^3/s)^2(1/in^5)
To:   psi
        * 43.533969
        / 0.022970568
```

The log includes conformability errors between the units at the 'You have:' and 'You want:' prompts, but not other errors, including lack of conformability of items in sums or differences or among items in a unit list. For example, a conversion between zenith angle and elevation angle could involve

```
You have: 90 deg - (5 deg + 22 min + 9 sec)
                                  ^

Illegal sum or difference of non-conformable units
You have: 90 deg - (5 deg + 22 arcmin + 9 arcsec)
You want: dms
          84 deg + 37 arcmin + 51 arcsec
You have: _
You want: deg
          * 84.630833
          / 0.011816024
You have:
```

The log file would contain

```
From: 90 deg - (5 deg + 22 arcmin + 9 arcsec)
To:   deg;arcmin;arcsec
          84 deg + 37 arcmin + 51 arcsec
From: _
To:   deg
          * 84.630833
          / 0.011816024
```

The initial entry error (forgetting that minutes have dimension of time, and that arcminutes must be used for dimensions of angle) does not appear in the output. When converting to a unit list alias, units expands the alias in the log file.

The 'From:' and 'To:' tags are written to the log file even if the '--quiet' option is given. If the log file exists when units is invoked, the new results are appended to the log file.

9 Invoking units

You invoke units like this:

units [options] [from-unit [to-unit]]

If the *from-unit* and *to-unit* are omitted, the program will use interactive prompts to determine which conversions to perform. See Chapter 2 [Interactive Use], page 1. If both *from-unit* and *to-unit* are given, units will print the result of that single conversion and then exit. If only *from-unit* appears on the command line, units will display the definition of that unit and exit. Units specified on the command line may need to be quoted to protect them from shell interpretation and to group them into two arguments. See Chapter 3 [Command Line Use], page 3.

The default behavior of units can be changed by various options given on the command line. In most cases, the options may be given in either short form (a single '-' followed by a single character) or long form ('--' followed by a word or hyphen-separated words). Short-form options are cryptic but require less typing; long-form options require more typing but are more explanatory and may be more mnemonic. With long-form options you need only enter sufficient characters to uniquely identify the option to the program. For example, '--out %f' works, but '--o %f' fails because units has other long options beginning with 'o'. However, '--q' works because '--quiet' is the only long option beginning with 'q'.

Some options require arguments to specify a value (e.g., '-d 12' or '--digits 12'). Short-form options that do not take arguments may be concatenated (e.g., '-erS' is equivalent to '-e -r -S'); the last option in such a list may be one that takes an argument (e.g., '-ed 12'). With short-form options, the space between an option and its argument is optional (e.g., '-d12' is equivalent to '-d 12'). Long-form options may not be concatenated, and the space between a long-form option and its argument is required. Short-form and long-form options may be intermixed on the command line. Options may be given in any order, but when incompatible options (e.g., '--output-format' and '--exponential') are given in combination behavior is controlled by the last option given. For example, '-o%.12f -e' gives exponential format with the default eight significant digits).

The following options are available:

-c

--check   Check that all units and prefixes defined in the units data file reduce to primitive units. Print a list of all units that cannot be reduced. Also display some other diagnostics about suspicious definitions in the units data file. Only definitions active in the current locale are checked. You should always run **units** with this option after modifying a units data file.

--check-verbose

--verbose-check

           Like the '--check' option, this option prints a list of units that cannot be reduced. But to help find unit definitions that cause endless loops, it lists the units as they are checked. If **units** hangs, then the last unit to be printed has a bad definition. Only definitions active in the current locale are checked.

-d ndigits

--digits ndigits

           Set the number of significant digits in the output to the value specified (which must be greater than zero). For example, '-d 12' sets the number of significant digits to 12. With exponential output **units** displays one digit to the left of the decimal point[2] and eleven digits to the right of the decimal point. On most systems, the maximum number of internally meaningful digits is 15: if you specify a greater number than your system's maximum, **units** will print a warning and set the number to the largest meaningful value. To directly set the maximum value, give an argument of **max** (e.g., '-d max'). Be aware, of course, that "significant" here refers only to the *display* of numbers; if results depend on physical constants not known to this precision, the physically meaningful precision may be less than that shown. The '--digits' option conflicts with the '--output-format' option.

-e

--exponential

           Set the numeric output format to exponential (i.e., scientific notation), like that used in the Unix **units** program. The default precision is eight significant

---

[2] This document refers to "decimal point," but strictly, the *radix* separates the integer and fractional parts of a floating-point number; in English-speaking countries, the radix is a point ('.'), but in most other countries it is a comma (',').

digits (seven digits to the right of the decimal point); this can be changed with the '--digits' option. The '--exponential' option conflicts with the '--output-format' option.

-o *format*
--output-format *format*

This option affords complete control over the numeric output format using the specified *format*. The format is a single floating point numeric format for the printf() function in the C programming language. All compilers support the format types 'g' and 'G' to specify significant digits, 'e' and 'E' for scientific notation, and 'f' for fixed-point decimal. The ISO C99 standard introduced the 'F' type for fixed-point decimal and the 'a' and 'A' types for hexadecimal floating point; these types are allowed with compilers that support them. The default format is '%.8g'; for greater precision, you could specify '-o %.15g'. See Chapter 11 [Numeric Output Format], page 31, and the documentation for printf() for more detailed descriptions of the format specification. The '--output-format' option affords the greatest control of the output appearance, but requires at least rudimentary knowledge of the printf() format syntax. If you don't want to bother with the printf() syntax, you can specify greater precision more simply with the '--digits' option or select exponential format with '--exponential'. The '--output-format' option is incompatible with the '--exponential' and '--digits' options.

-f *filename*
--file *filename*

Instruct units to load the units file *filename*. You can specify up to 25 units files on the command line. When you use this option, units will load *only* the files you list on the command line; it will not load the standard file or your personal units file unless you explicitly list them. If *filename* is the empty string ('-f ""'), the default units file (or that specified by UNITSFILE) will be loaded in addition to any others specified with '-f'.

-L *logfile*
--log *logfile*

Save the results of calculations in the file *logfile*; this can be useful if it is important to have a record of unit conversions or other calculations that are to be used extensively or in a critical activity such as a program or design project. If *logfile* exits, the new results are appended to the file. See Chapter 8 [Logging Calculations], page 19, for a more detailed description and some examples.

-h
--help   Print out a summary of the options for units.

-m
--minus   Causes '-' to be interpreted as a subtraction operator. This is the default behavior.

`-p`

`--product`

Causes '-' to be interpreted as a multiplication operator when it has two operands. It will act as a negation operator when it has only one operand: '(-3)'. By default '-' is treated as a subtraction operator.

`--oldstar`

Causes '*' to have the old-style precedence, higher than the precedence of division so that '1/2*3' will equal '1/6'.

`--newstar`

Forces '*' to have the new (default) precedence that follows the usual rules of algebra: the precedence of '*' is the same as the precedence of '/', so that '1/2*3' will equal '3/2'.

`--compact`

Give compact output featuring only the conversion factor. This turns off the '--verbose' option.

`-q`

`--quiet`

`--silent`   Suppress prompting of the user for units and the display of statistics about the number of units loaded.

`-n`

`--nolists`

Disable conversion to unit lists.

`-r`

`--round`   When converting to a combination of units given by a unit list, round the value of the last unit in the list to the nearest integer.

`-S`

`--show-factor`

When converting to a combination of units specified in a list, always show a non-unity factor before a unit that begins with a fraction with a unity denominator. By default, if the unit in a list begins with fraction of the form 1|x and its multiplier is an integer other than 1, the fraction is given as the product of the multiplier and the numerator (e.g., '3|8 in' rather than '3 * 1|8 in'). In some cases, this is not what is wanted; for example, the results for a cooking recipe might show '3 * 1|2 cup' as '3|2 cup'. With the '--show-factor' option, a result equivalent to 1.5 cups will display as '3 * 1|2 cup' rather than '3|2 cup'. A user-specified fractional unit with a numerator other than 1 is never overridden, however—if a unit list specifies '3|4 cup;1|2 cup', a result equivalent to 1 1/2 cups will always be shown as '2 * 3|4 cup' whether or not the '--show-factor' option is given.

`-s`

`--strict`   Suppress conversion of units to their reciprocal units. For example, units will normally convert hertz to seconds because these units are reciprocals of each other. The strict option requires that units be strictly conformable to perform a conversion, and will give an error if you attempt to convert hertz to seconds.

`-1`
`--one-line`

> Give only one line of output (the forward conversion). Do not print the reverse conversion. If a reciprocal conversion is performed then **units** will still print the "reciprocal conversion" line.

`-t`
`--terse`   Give terse output when converting units. This option can be used when calling **units** from another program so that the output is easy to parse. This option has the combined effect of these options: '`--strict`' '`--quiet`' '`--one-line`' '`--compact`'. When combined with '`--version`' it produces a display showing only the program name and version number.

`-v`
`--verbose`

> Give slightly more verbose output when converting units. When combined with the '`-c`' option this gives the same effect as '`--check-verbose`'. When combined with '`--version`' produces a more detailed output, equivalent to the '`--info`' option.

`-V`
`--version`

> Print the program version number, tell whether the **readline** library has been included, tell whether UTF-8 support has been included; give the locale, the location of the default units data file, and the location of the personal units data file; indicate if the personal units data file does not exist.

> When given in combination with the '`--terse`' option, the program prints only the version number and exits.

> When given in combination with the '`--verbose`' option, the program, the '`--version`' option has the same effect as the '`--info`' option below.

`-I`
`--info`   Print the information given with the '`--version`' option, show the pathname of the units program, show the status of the UNITSFILE and MYUNITSFILE environment variables, and additional information about how **units** locates the related files. On systems running Microsoft Windows, the status of the UNITSLOCALE environment variable and information about the related locale map are also given. This option is usually of interest only to developers and administrators, but it can sometimes be useful for troubleshooting.

> Combining the '`--version`' and '`--verbose`' options has the same effect as giving '`--info`'.

`-U`
`--unitsfile`

> Print the location of the default units data file and exit; if the file cannot be found, print "Units data file not found".

```
-l locale
--locale locale
```
> Print the information given with the '--version' option, show the Force a specified locale such as 'en_GB' to get British definitions by default. This over-rides the locale determined from system settings or environment variables. See Section 12.1 [Locale], page 34, for a description of locale format.

10 Adding Your Own Definitions

10.1 Units Data Files

The units and prefixes that **units** can convert are defined in the units data file, typically '/usr/share/units/definitions.units'. If you can't find this file, run **units --version** to get information on the file locations for your installation. Although you can extend or modify this data file if you have appropriate user privileges, it's usually better to put extensions in separate files so that the definitions will be preserved if you update **units**.

You can include additional data files in the units database using the '!include' command in the standard units data file. For example

```
!include     /usr/local/share/units/local.units
```

might be appropriate for a site-wide supplemental data file. The location of the '!include' statement in the standard units data file is important; later definitions replace earlier ones, so any definitions in an included file will override definitions before the '!include' state-ment in the standard units data file. With normal invocation, no warning is given about redefinitions; to ensure that you don't have an unintended redefinition, run **units -c** after making changes to any units data file.

If you want to add your own units in addition to or in place of standard or site-wide supplemental units data files, you can include them in the '.units' file in your home direc-tory. If this file exists it is read after the standard units data file, so that any definitions in this file will replace definitions of the same units in the standard data file or in files included from the standard data file. This file will not be read if any units files are specified on the command line. (Under Windows the personal units file is named 'unitdef.units'.) Running **units -V** will display the location and name of your personal units file.

The **units** program first tries to determine your home directory from the HOME envi-ronment variable. On systems running Microsoft Windows, if HOME does not exist, **units** attempts to find your home directory from HOMEDRIVE, HOMEPATH and USERPROFILE. You can specify an arbitrary file as your personal units data file with the MYUNITSFILE environ-ment variable; if this variable exists its value is used without searching your home directory. The default units data files are described in more detail in Chapter 14 [Data Files], page 37.

10.2 Defining New Units and Prefixes

A unit is specified on a single line by giving its name and an equivalence. Comments start with a '#' character, which can appear anywhere in a line. The backslash character ('\') acts as a continuation character if it appears as the last character on a line, making it possible to spread definitions out over several lines if desired. A file can be included by giving the command '`!include`' followed by the file's name. The '`!`' must be the first character on the line. The file will be sought in the same directory as the parent file unless you give a full path. The name of the file to be included cannot contain the comment character '`#`'.

Unit names must not contain any of the operator characters '`+`', '`-`', '`*`', '`/`', '`|`', '`^`', '`;`', '`~`', the comment character '`#`', or parentheses. They cannot begin or end with an underscore ('`_`'), a comma ('`,`') or a decimal point ('`.`'). The figure dash (U+2012), typographical minus ('`−`'; U+2212), and en dash ('`–`'; U+2013) are converted to the operator '`-`', so none of these characters can appear in unit names. Names cannot begin with a digit, and if a name ends in a digit other than zero, the digit must be preceded by a string beginning with an underscore, and afterwards consisting only of digits, decimal points, or commas. For example, '`foo_2`', '`foo_2,1`', or '`foo_3.14`' are valid names but '`foo2`' or '`foo_a2`' are invalid. You could define nitrous oxide as

```
N2O      nitrogen 2  + oxygen
```

but would need to define nitrogen dioxide as

```
NO_2     nitrogen + oxygen 2
```

Be careful to define new units in terms of old ones so that a reduction leads to the primitive units, which are marked with '`!`' characters. Dimensionless units are indicated by using the string '`!dimensionless`' for the unit definition.

When adding new units, be sure to use the '`-c`' option to check that the new units reduce properly. If you create a loop in the units definitions, then **units** will hang when invoked with the '`-c`' option. You will need to use the '`--check-verbose`' option, which prints out each unit as it is checked. The program will still hang, but the last unit printed will be the unit that caused the infinite loop.

If you define any units that contain '`+`' characters, carefully check them because the '`-c`' option will not catch non-conformable sums. Be careful with the '`-`' operator as well. When used as a binary operator, the '`-`' character can perform addition or multiplication depending on the options used to invoke **units**. To ensure consistent behavior use '`-`' only as a unary negation operator when writing units definitions. To multiply two units leave a space or use the '`*`' operator with care, recalling that it has two possible precedence values and may require parentheses to ensure consistent behavior. To compute the difference of '`foo`' and '`bar`' write '`foo+(-bar)`' or even '`foo+-bar`'.

Here is an example of a short data file that defines some basic units:

```
m         !               # The meter is a primitive unit
sec       !               # The second is a primitive unit
rad       !dimensionless  # A dimensionless primitive unit
micro-    1e-6            # Define a prefix
minute    60 sec          # A minute is 60 seconds
hour      60 min          # An hour is 60 minutes
inch      0.0254 m        # Inch defined in terms of meters
ft        12 inches       # The foot defined in terms of inches
mile      5280 ft         # And the mile
```

A unit that ends with a '`-`' character is a prefix. If a prefix definition contains any '`/`' characters, be sure they are protected by parentheses. If you define '`half- 1/2`' then '`halfmeter`' would be equivalent to '`1 / (2 meter)`'.

10.3 Defining Nonlinear Units

Some unit conversions of interest are nonlinear; for example, temperature conversions between the Fahrenheit and Celsius scales cannot be done by simply multiplying by conversion factors.

When you give a linear unit definition such as 'inch 2.54 cm' you are providing information that units uses to convert values in inches into primitive units of meters. For nonlinear units, you give a functional definition that provides the same information.

Nonlinear units are represented using a functional notation. It is best to regard this notation not as a function call but as a way of adding units to a number, much the same way that writing a linear unit name after a number adds units to that number. Internally, nonlinear units are defined by a pair of functions that convert to and from linear units in the database, so that an eventual conversion to primitive units is possible.

Here is an example nonlinear unit definition:

```
tempF(x) units=[1;K] domain=[-459.67,) range=[0,) \
        (x+(-32)) degF + stdtemp ; (tempF+(-stdtemp))/degF + 32
```

A nonlinear unit definition comprises a unit name, a formal parameter name, two functions, and optional specifications for units, the domain, and the range (the domain of the inverse function). The functions tell units how to convert to and from the new unit. To produce valid results, the arguments of these functions need to have the correct dimensions and be within the domains for which the functions are defined.

The definition begins with the unit name followed immediately (with no spaces) by a '(' character. In the parentheses is the name of the formal parameter. Next is an optional specification of the units required by the functions in the definition. In the example above, the 'units=[1;K]' specification indicates that the 'tempF' function requires an input argument conformable with '1' (i.e., the argument is dimensionless), and that the inverse function requires an input argument conformable with 'K'. For normal nonlinear units definition, the forward function will always take a dimensionless argument; in general, the inverse function will need units that match the quantity measured by your nonlinear unit. Specifying the units enables units to perform error checking on function arguments, and also to assign units to domain and range specifications, which are described later.

Next the function definitions appear. In the example above, the 'tempF' function is defined by

```
tempF(x) = (x+(-32)) degF + stdtemp
```

This gives a rule for converting 'x' in the units 'tempF' to linear units of absolute temperature, which makes it possible to convert from tempF to other units.

To enable conversions to Fahrenheit, you must give a rule for the inverse conversions. The inverse will be 'x(tempF)' and its definition appears after a ';' character. In our example, the inverse is

```
x(tempF) = (tempF+(-stdtemp))/degF + 32
```

This inverse definition takes an absolute temperature as its argument and converts it to the Fahrenheit temperature. The inverse can be omitted by leaving out the ';' character and the inverse definition, but then conversions *to* the unit will not be possible. If the inverse definition is omitted, the '--check' option will display a warning. It is up to you to calculate and enter the correct inverse function to obtain proper conversions; the '--check' option tests the inverse at one point and prints an error if it is not valid there, but this is not a guarantee that your inverse is correct.

With some definitions, the units may vary. For example, the definition

```
square(x)        x^2
```

can have any arbitrary units, and can also take dimensionless arguments. In such a case, you should *not* specify units. If a definition takes a root of its arguments, the definition is valid only for units that yield such a root. For example,

```
squirt(x)        sqrt(x)
```

is valid for a dimensionless argument, and for arguments with even powers of units.

Some definitions may not be valid for all real numbers. In such cases, **units** can handle errors better if you specify an appropriate domain and range. You specify the domain and range as shown below:

```
baume(d) units=[1;g/cm^3] domain=[0,130.5] range=[1,10] \
         (145/(145-d)) g/cm^3 ; (baume+-g/cm^3) 145 / baume
```

In this example the domain is specified after 'domain=' with the endpoints given in brackets. In accord with mathematical convention, square brackets indicate a closed interval (one that includes its endpoints), and parentheses indicate an open interval (one that does not include its endpoints). An interval can be open or closed on one or both ends; an interval that is unbounded on either end is indicated by omitting the limit on that end. For example, a quantity to which decibel (dB) is applied may have any value greater than zero, so the range is indicated by '(0,)':

```
decibel(x) units=[1;1] range=(0,) 10^(x/10); 10 log(decibel)
```

If the domain or range is given, the second endpoint must be greater than the first.

The domain and range specifications can appear independently and in any order along with the units specification. The values for the domain and range endpoints are attached to the units given in the units specification, and if necessary, the parameter value is adjusted for comparison with the endpoints. For example, if a definition includes 'units=[1;ft]' and 'range=[3,)', the range will be taken as 3 ft to infinity. If the function is passed a parameter of '900 mm', that value will be adjusted to 2.9527559 ft, which is outside the specified range. If you omit the units specification from the previous example, **units** can not tell whether you intend the lower endpoint to be 3 ft or 3 microfurlongs, and can not adjust the parameter value of 900 mm for comparison. Without units, numerical values other than zero or plus or minus infinity for domain or range endpoints are meaningless, and accordingly they are not allowed. If you give other values without units then the definition will be ignored and you will get an error message.

Although the units, domain, and range specifications are optional, it's best to give them when they are applicable; doing so allows **units** to perform better error checking and give more helpful error messages. Giving the domain and range also enables the '--check' option to find a point in the domain to use for its point check of your inverse definition.

You can make synonyms for nonlinear units by providing both the forward and inverse functions; inverse functions can be obtained using the '~' operator. So to create a synonym for 'tempF' you could write

```
fahrenheit(x) units=[1;K] tempF(x); ~tempF(fahrenheit)
```

This is useful for creating a nonlinear unit definition that differs slightly from an existing definition without having to repeat the original functions. For example,

```
dBW(x)      units=[1;W] range=[0,) dB(x) W ;   ~dB(dBW/W)
```

If you wish a synonym to refer to an existing nonlinear unit without modification, you can do so more simply by adding the synonym with appended parentheses as a new unit, with the existing nonlinear unit—without parentheses—as the definition. So to create a synonym for 'tempF' you could write

```
fahrenheit()   tempF
```

The definition must be a nonlinear unit; for example, the synonym

```
fahrenheit()   meter
```

will result in an error message when **units** starts.

You may occasionally wish to define a function that operates on units. This can be done using a nonlinear unit definition. For example, the definition below provides conversion between radius and the area of a circle. This definition requires a length as input and produces an area as output, as indicated by the '**units=**' specification. Specifying the range as the nonnegative numbers can prevent cryptic error messages.

```
circlearea(r) units=[m;m^2] range=[0,)   pi r^2 ; sqrt(circlearea/pi)
```

10.4 Defining Piecewise Linear Units

Sometimes you may be interested in a piecewise linear unit such as many wire gauges. Piecewise linear units can be defined by specifying conversions to linear units on a list of points. Conversion at other points will be done by linear interpolation. A partial definition of zinc gauge is

```
zincgauge[in] 1 0.002, 10 0.02, 15 0.04, 19 0.06, 23 0.1
```

In this example, 'zincgauge' is the name of the piecewise linear unit. The definition of such a unit is indicated by the embedded '[' character. After the bracket, you should indicate the units to be attached to the numbers in the table. No spaces can appear before the ']' character, so a definition like '**foo[kg meters]**' is invalid; instead write '**foo[kg*meters]**'. The definition of the unit consists of a list of pairs optionally separated by commas. This list defines a function for converting from the piecewise linear unit to linear units. The first item in each pair is the function argument; the second item is the value of the function at that argument (in the units specified in brackets). In this example, we define '**zincgauge**' at five points. For example, we set '**zincgauge(1)**' equal to '0.002 in'. Definitions like this may be more readable if written using continuation characters as

```
zincgauge[in] \
    1 0.002  \
   10 0.02   \
   15 0.04   \
   19 0.06   \
   23 0.1
```

With the preceding definition, the following conversion can be performed:

```
You have: zincgauge(10)
You want: in
    * 0.02
    / 50
You have: .01 inch
You want: zincgauge
    5
```

If you define a piecewise linear unit that is not strictly monotonic, then the inverse will not be well defined. If the inverse is requested for such a unit, **units** will return the smallest inverse.

After adding nonlinear units definitions, you should normally run **units --check** to check for errors. If the 'units' keyword is not given, the '--check' option checks a nonlinear unit definition using a dimensionless argument, and then checks using an arbitrary combination of units, as well as the square and cube of that combination; a warning is given if any of these tests fail. For example,

```
Warning: function 'squirt(x)' defined as 'sqrt(x)'
         failed for some test inputs:
         squirt(7(kg K)^1): Unit not a root
         squirt(7(kg K)^3): Unit not a root
```

Running **units --check** will print a warning if a non-monotonic piecewise linear unit is encountered. For example, the relationship between ANSI coated abrasive designation and mean particle size is non-monotonic in the vicinity of 800 grit:

```
ansicoated[micron] \

    . . .
    600 10.55 \
    800 11.5 \
    1000 9.5 \
```

Running **units --check** would give the error message

```
Table 'ansicoated' lacks unique inverse around entry 800
```

Although the inverse is not well defined in this region, it's not really an error. Viewing such error messages can be tedious, and if there are enough of them, they can distract from true errors. Error checking for nonlinear unit definitions can be suppressed by giving the 'noerror' keyword; for the examples above, this could be done as

```
squirt(x) noerror domain=[0,) range=[0,) sqrt(x); squirt^2
ansicoated[micron] noerror \

    . . .
```

Use the 'noerror' keyword with caution. The safest approach after adding a nonlinear unit definition is to run **units --check** and confirm that there are no actual errors before adding the 'noerror' keyword.

10.5 Defining Unit List Aliases

Unit list aliases are treated differently from unit definitions, because they are a data entry shorthand rather than a true definition for a new unit. A unit list alias definition begins with '!unitlist' and includes the alias and the definition; for example, the aliases included in the standard units data file are

```
!unitlist    hms      hr;min;sec
!unitlist    time     year;day;hr;min;sec
!unitlist    dms      deg;arcmin;arcsec
!unitlist    ftin     ft;in;1|8 in
!unitlist    usvol    cup;3|4 cup;2|3 cup;1|2 cup;1|3 cup;1|4 cup;\
                      tbsp;tsp;1|2 tsp;1|4 tsp;1|8 tsp
```

Unit list aliases are only for unit lists, so the definition must include a ';'. Unit list aliases can never be combined with units or other unit list aliases, so the definition of 'time' shown above could *not* have been shortened to 'year;day;hms'.

As usual, be sure to run units --check to ensure that the units listed in unit list aliases are conformable.

11 Numeric Output Format

By default, units shows results to eight significant digits. You can change this with the '--exponential', '--digits', and '--output-format' options. The first sets an exponential format (i.e., scientific notation) like that used in the original Unix units program, the second allows you to specify a different number of significant digits, and the last allows you to control the output appearance using the format for the printf() function in the C programming language. If you only want to change the number of significant digits or specify exponential format type, use the '--digits' and '--exponential' options. The '--output-format' option affords the greatest control of the output appearance, but requires at least rudimentary knowledge of the printf() format syntax. See Chapter 9 [Invoking Units], page 20, for descriptions of these options.

11.1 Format Specification

The format specification recognized with the '--output-format' option is a subset of that for printf(). The format specification has the form %[*flags*][*width*][.*precision*]*type*; it must begin with '%', and must end with a floating-point type specifier: 'g' or 'G' to specify the number of significant digits, 'e' or 'E' for scientific notation, and 'f' for fixed-point decimal. The ISO C99 standard added the 'F' type for fixed-point decimal and the 'a' and 'A' types for hexadecimal floating point; these types are allowed with compilers that support them. Type length modifiers (e.g., 'L' to indicate a long double) are inapplicable and are not allowed.

The default format for units is '%.8g'; for greater precision, you could specify '-o %.15g'. The 'g' and 'G' format types use exponential format whenever the exponent would be less than −4, so the value 0.000013 displays as '1.3e-005'. These types also use exponential notation when the exponent is greater than or equal to the precision, so with the default format, the value 5×10^7 displays as '50000000' and the value 5×10^8 displays as '5e+008'. If you prefer fixed-point display, you might specify '-o %.8f'; however, small numbers will display very few significant digits, and values less than 0.5×10^{-8} will show nothing but zeros.

The format specification may include one or more optional flags: '+', ' ' (space), '#', '-', or '0' (the digit zero). The digit-grouping flag ' '' (apostrophe) is allowed with compilers that support it. Flags are followed by an optional value for the minimum field width, and an optional precision specification that begins with a period (e.g., '.6'). The field width includes the digits, decimal point, the exponent, thousands separators (with the digit-grouping flag), and the sign if any of these are shown.

11.2 Flags

The '+' flag causes the output to have a sign ('+' or '-'). The space flag ' ' is similar to the '+' flag, except that when the value is positive, it is prefixed with a space rather than a plus sign; this flag is ignored if the '+' flag is also given. The '+' or ' ' flag could be useful if conversions might include positive and negative results, and you wanted to align the decimal points in exponential notation. The '#' flag causes the output value to contain a decimal point in all cases; by default, the output contains a decimal point only if there are digits (which can be trailing zeros) to the right of the point. With the 'g' or 'G' types, the '#' flag also prevents the suppression of trailing zeros. The digit-grouping flag ' '' shows a thousands separator in digits to the left of the decimal point. This can be useful when displaying large numbers in fixed-point decimal; for example, with the format '%f',

```
You have: mile
You want: microfurlong
        * 8000000.000000
        / 0.000000
```

the magnitude of the first result may not be immediately obvious without counting the digits to the left of the decimal point. If the thousands separator is the comma (','), the output with the format '%'f' might be

```
You have: mile
You want: microfurlong
        * 8,000,000.000000
        / 0.000000
```

making the magnitude readily apparent. Unfortunately, few compilers support the digit-grouping flag.

With the '-' flag, the output value is left aligned within the specified field width. If a field width greater than needed to show the output value is specified, the '0' (zero) flag causes the output value to be left padded with zeros until the specified field width is reached; for example, with the format '%011.6f',

```
You have: troypound
You want: grain
        * 5760.000000
        / 0000.000174
```

The '0' flag has no effect if the '-' (left align) flag is given.

11.3 Field Width

By default, the output value is left aligned and shown with the minimum width necessary for the specified (or default) precision. If a field width greater than this is specified, the value shown is right aligned, and padded on the left with enough spaces to provide the specified field width. A width specification is typically used with fixed-point decimal to have columns of numbers align at the decimal point; this arguably is less useful with units than with long columnar output, but it may nonetheless assist in quickly assessing the relative magnitudes of results. For example, with the format '%12.6f',

```
You have: km
You want: in
        * 39370.078740
        /     0.000025
You have: km
You want: rod
        *   198.838782
        /     0.005029
You have: km
You want: furlong
        *     4.970970
        /     0.201168
```

11.4 Precision

The meaning of "precision" depends on the format type. With 'g' or 'G', it specifies the number of significant digits (like the '--digits' option); with 'e', 'E', 'f', or 'F', it specifies the maximum number of digits to be shown after the decimal point.

With the 'g' and 'G' format types, trailing zeros are suppressed, so the results may sometimes have fewer digits than the specified precision (as indicated above, the '#' flag causes trailing zeros to be displayed).

The default precision is 6, so '%g' is equivalent to '%.6g', and would show the output to six significant digits. Similarly, '%e' or '%f' would show the output with six digits after the decimal point.

The C printf() function allows a precision of arbitrary size, whether or not all of the digits are meaningful. With most compilers, the maximum internal precision with units is 15 decimal digits (or 13 hexadecimal digits). With the '--digits' option, you are limited to the maximum internal precision; with the '--output-format' option, you may specify a precision greater than this, but it may not be meaningful. In some cases, specifying excess precision can result in rounding artifacts. For example, a pound is exactly 7000 grains, but with the format '%.18g', the output might be

```
You have: pound
You want: grain
        * 6999.9999999999991
        / 0.000142857142857142857
```

With the format '%.25g' you might get the following:

```
You have: 1/3
You want:
        Definition: 0.3333333333333333148296616256247
```

In this case the displayed value includes a series of digits that represent the underlying binary floating-point approximation to 1/3 but are not meaningful for the desired computation.

In general, the result with excess precision is system dependent. The precision affects only the *display* of numbers; if a result relies on physical constants that are not known to the specified precision, the number of physically meaningful digits may be less than the number of digits shown.

See the documentation for `printf()` for more detailed descriptions of the format specification.

The '`--output-format`' option is incompatible with the '`--exponential`' or '`--digits`' options; if the former is given in combination with either of the latter, the format is controlled by the last option given.

12 Localization

Some units have different values in different locations. The localization feature accommodates this by allowing a units data file to specify definitions that depend on the user's locale.

12.1 Locale

A locale is a subset of a user's environment that indicates the user's language and country, and some attendant preferences, such as the formatting of dates. The **units** program attempts to determine the locale from the POSIX setlocale function; if this cannot be done, **units** examines the environment variables `LC_CTYPE` and `LANG`. On POSIX systems, a locale is of the form *language_country*, where *language* is the two-character code from ISO 639-1 and *country* is the two-character code from ISO 3166-1; *language* is lower case and *country* is upper case. For example, the POSIX locale for the United Kingdom is `en_GB`.

On systems running Microsoft Windows, the value returned by setlocale() is different from that on POSIX systems; **units** attempts to map the Windows value to a POSIX value by means of a table in the file '`locale_map.txt`' in the same directory as the other data files. The file includes entries for many combinations of language and country, and can be extended to include other combinations. The '`locale_map.txt`' file comprises two tab-separated columns; each entry is of the form

> *Windows-locale   POSIX-locale*

where *POSIX-locale* is as described above, and *Windows-locale* typically spells out both the language and country. For example, the entry for the United States is

```
English_United States    en_US
```

You can force **units** to run in a desired locale by using the '`-l`' option.

In order to create unit definitions for a particular locale you begin a block of definitions in a unit datafile with '`!locale`' followed by a locale name. The '`!`' must be the first character on the line. The **units** program reads the following definitions only if the current locale matches. You end the block of localized units with '`!endlocale`'. Here is an example, which defines the British gallon.

```
!locale en_GB
gallon        4.54609 liter
!endlocale
```

12.2 Additional Localization

Sometimes the locale isn't sufficient to determine unit preferences. There could be regional preferences, or a company could have specific preferences. Though probably uncommon, such differences could arise with the choice of English customary units outside of English-speaking countries. To address this, **units** allows specifying definitions that depend on environment variable settings. The environment variables can be controled based on the current locale, or the user can set them to force a particular group of definitions.

A conditional block of definitions in a units data file begins with either '**!var** or '**!varnot**' following by an environment variable name and then a space separated list of values. The leading '!' must appear in the first column of a units data file, and the conditional block is terminated by '**!endvar**'. Definitions in blocks beginning with '**!var**' are executed only if the environment variable is exactly equal to one of the listed values. Definitions in blocks beginning with '**!varnot**' are executed only if the environment variable does *not* equal any of the list values.

The inch has long been a customary measure of length in many places. The word comes from the latin *uncia* meaning "one twelfth," referring to its relationship with the foot. By the 20th century, the inch was officially defined in English-speaking countries relative to the yard, but until 1959, the yard differed slightly among those countries. In France the customary inch, which was displaced in 1799 by the meter, had a different length based on a french foot. These customary definitions could be accommodated as follows:

```
!var INCH_UNIT usa
yard            3600|3937 m
!endvar
!var INCH_UNIT canada
yard            0.9144 meter
!endvar
!var INCH_UNIT uk
yard            0.91439841 meter
!endvar
!var INCH_UNIT canada uk usa
foot            1|3 yard
inch            1|12 foot
!endvar
!var INCH_UNIT france
foot            144|443.296 m
inch            1|12 foot
line            1|12 inch
!endvar
!varnot INCH_UNIT usa uk france canada
!message Unknown value for INCH_UNIT
!endvar
```

When **units** reads the above definitions it will check the environment variable `INCH_UNIT` and load only the definitions for the appropriate section. If `INCH_UNIT` is unset or is not set to one of the four values listed then **units** will run the last block. In this case that block uses the '!message' command to display a warning message. Alternatively that block could set default values.

In order to create default values that are overridden by user settings the data file can use the '!set' command, which sets an environment variable *only if it is not already set*; these settings are only for the current **units** invocation and do not persist. So if the example above were preceded by '!set INCH_UNIT france' then this would make 'france' the default value for INCH_UNIT. If the user had set the variable in the environment before invoking **units**, then **units** would use the user's value.

To link these settings to the user's locale you combine the '!set' command with the '!locale' command. If you wanted to combine the above example with suitable locales you could do by *preceding* the above definition with the following:

```
!locale en_US
!set INCH_UNIT usa
!endlocale
!locale en_GB
!set INCH_UNIT uk
!endlocale
!locale en_CA
!set INCH_UNIT canada
!endlocale
!locale fr_FR
!set INCH_UNIT france
!endlocale
!set INCH_UNIT france
```

These definitions set the overall default for INCH_UNIT to 'france' and set default values for four locales appropriately. The overall default setting comes last so that it only applies when INCH_UNIT was not set by one of the other commands or by the user.

If the variable given after '!var' or '!varnot' is undefined then **units** prints an error message and ignores the definitions that follow. Use '!set' to create defaults to prevent this situation from arising. The '-c' option only checks the definitions that are active for the current environment and locale, so when adding new definitions take care to check that all cases give rise to a well defined set of definitions.

13 Environment Variables

The **units** program uses the following environment variables:

HOME   Specifies the location of your home directory; it is used by **units** to find a personal units data file '.units'. On systems running Microsoft Windows, the file is 'unitdef.units', and if HOME does not exist, **units** tries to determine your home directory from the HOMEDRIVE and HOMEPATH environment variables; if these variables do not exist, units finally tries USERPROFILE—typically 'C:\Users*username*' (Windows Vista and Windows 7) or 'C:\Documents and Settings*username*' (Windows XP).

LC_CTYPE, LANG
>   Checked to determine the locale if **units** cannot obtain it from the operating system. Sections of the standard units data file are specific to certain locales.

MYUNITSFILE
>   Specifies your personal units data file. If this variable exists, **units** uses its value rather than searching your home directory for '.units'. The personal units file will not be loaded if any data files are given using the '-f' option.

PAGER   Specifies the pager to use for help and for displaying the conformable units. The help function browses the units database and calls the pager using the '+n'*n* syntax for specifying a line number. The default pager is **more**; PAGER can be used to specify alternatives such as **less**, **pg**, **emacs**, or **vi**.

UNITS_ENGLISH
>   Set to either 'US' or 'GB' to choose United States or British volume definitions, overriding the default from your locale.

UNITSFILE
>   Specifies the units data file to use (instead of the default). You can only specify a single units data file using this environment variable. If units data files are given using the '-f' option, the file specified by UNITSFILE will be not be loaded unless the '-f' option is given with the empty string ('**units -f ""**').

UNITSLOCALEMAP
>   Windows only; this variable has no effect on Unix-like systems. Specifies the units locale map file to use (instead of the default). This variable seldom needs to be set, but you can use it to ensure that the locale map file will be found if you specify a location for the units data file using either the '-f' option or the UNITSFILE environment variable, and that location does not also contain the locale map file.

14 Data Files

The **units** program uses two default data files: 'definitions.units' and 'currency.units'. The program can also use an optional personal units data file '.units' ('unitdef.units' under Windows) located in the user's home directory. The personal units data file is described in more detail in Section 10.1 [Units Data Files], page 25.

On Unix-like systems, the data files are typically located in '/usr/share/units' if **units** is provided with the operating system, or in '/usr/local/share/units' if **units** is compiled from the source distribution.

On systems running Microsoft Windows, the files may be in the same locations if Unix-like commands are available, a Unix-like file structure is present (e.g., 'C:/usr/local'), and **units** is compiled from the source distribution. If Unix-like commands are not available, a more common location is 'C:\Program Files (x86)\GNU\units' (for 64-bit Windows installations) or 'C:\Program Files\GNU\units' (for 32-bit installations).

If **units** is obtained from the GNU Win32 Project (http://gnuwin32.sourceforge.net/), the files are commonly in 'C:\Program Files\GnuWin32\share\units'.

If the default units data file is not an absolute pathname, `units` will look for the file in the directory that contains the `units` program; if the file is not found there, `units` will look in a directory `../share/units` relative to the directory with the `units` program.

You can determine the location of the files by running `units --version`. Running `units --info` will give you additional information about the files, how `units` will attempt to find them, and the status of the related environment variables.

15 Unicode Support

The standard units data file is in Unicode, using UTF-8 encoding. Most definitions use only ASCII characters (i.e., code points U+0000 through U+007F); definitions using non-ASCII characters appear in blocks beginning with '`!utf8`' and ending with '`!endutf8`'.

When `units` starts, it checks the locale to determine the character set. If `units` is compiled with Unicode support and definitions; otherwise these definitions are ignored. When Unicode support is active, `units` will check every line of all of the units data files for invalid or non-printing UTF-8 sequences; if such sequences occur, `units` ignores the entire line. In addition to checking validity, `units` determines the display width of non-ASCII characters to ensure proper positioning of the pointer in some error messages and to align columns for the '`search`' and '`?`' commands.

At present, `units` does not support Unicode under Microsoft Windows. The UTF-16 and UTF-32 encodings are not supported on any systems.

If definitions that contain non-ASCII characters are added to a units data file, those definitions should be enclosed within '`!utf8`' ... '`!endutf8`' to ensure that they are only loaded when Unicode support is available. As usual, the '`!`' must appear as the first character on the line. As discussed in Section 10.1 [Units Data Files], page 25, it's usually best to put such definitions in supplemental data files linked by an '`!include`' command or in a personal units data file.

When Unicode support is not active, `units` makes no assumptions about character encoding, except that characters in the range 00–7F hexadecimal correspond to ASCII encoding. Non-ASCII characters are simply sequences of bytes, and have no special meanings; for definitions in supplementary units data files, you can use any encoding consistent with this assumption. For example, if you wish to use non-ASCII characters in definitions when running `units` under Windows, you can use a character set such as Windows "ANSI" (code page 1252 in the US and Western Europe). You can even use UTF-8, though some messages may be improperly aligned, and `units` will not detect invalid UTF-8 sequences. If you use UTF-8 encoding when Unicode support is not active, you should place any definitions with non-ASCII characters *outside* '`!utf8`' ... '`!endutf8`' blocks—otherwise, they will be ignored.

Typeset material other than code examples usually uses the Unicode minus (U+2212) rather than the ASCII hyphen-minus operator (U+002D) used in `units`; the figure dash (U+2012) and en dash (U+2013) are also occasionally used. To allow such material to be copied and pasted for interactive use or in units data files, `units` converts these characters to U+002D before further processing. Because of this, none of these characters can appear in unit names.

16 Readline Support

If the `readline` package has been compiled in, then when `units` is used interactively, numerous command line editing features are available. To check if your version of `units` includes `readline`, invoke the program with the '`--version`' option.

For complete information about `readline`, consult the documentation for the `readline` package. Without any configuration, `units` will allow editing in the style of emacs. Of particular use with `units` are the completion commands.

If you type a few characters and then hit ESC followed by `?` then `units` will display a list of all the units that start with the characters typed. For example, if you type *metr* and then request completion, you will see something like this:

```
You have: metr
metre             metriccup          metrichorsepower   metrictenth
metretes          metricfifth        metricounce        metricton
metriccarat       metricgrain        metricquart        metricyarncount
You have: metr
```

If there is a unique way to complete a unitname, you can hit the TAB key and `units` will provide the rest of the unit name. If `units` beeps, it means that there is no unique completion. Pressing the TAB key a second time will print the list of all completions.

17 Updating Currency Exchange Rates

The units program includes currency exchange rates and prices for some precious metals in the database. Of course, these values change over time, sometimes very rapidly, and `units` cannot provide real time values. To update the exchange rates run the `units_cur`, which rewrites the files containing the currency rates, typically '`/usr/share/units/currency.units`'. This program requires `python` and the `unidecode` package, and must be run with suitable permissions to write the file. To keep the rates updated automatically, run it using a cron job on a Unix-like system, or a similar scheduling program on a different system. Currency exchange rates are taken from Time Genie (`http://www.timegenie.com`) and precious metals pricing from Packetizer (`www.packetizer.com`). These sites update once per day, so there is no benefit in running the update script more often than daily. You can run `units_cur` with a filename specified on the command line and it will write the data to that file. If you give '`-`' for the file it will write to standard output.

18 Database Command Syntax

unit definition
> Define a regular unit.

prefix- definition
> Define a prefix.

`funcname(var)` noerror `units=[in-units,out-units]` `domain=[x1,x2]`
`range=[y1,y2]` `definition(var)` ; `inverse(funcname)`
> Define a nonlinear unit or unit function. The four optional keywords **noerror**, **units=**, **range=** and **domain=** can appear in any order. The definition of the inverse is optional.

`tabname[out-units]` noerror `pair-list`
> Define a piecewise linear unit. The pair list gives the points on the table listed in ascending order. The **noerror** keyword is optional.

`!endlocale`
> End a block of definitions beginning with '`!locale`'

`!endutf8`   End a block of definitions begun with '`!utf8`'

`!endvar`   End a block of definitions begun with '`!var`' or '`!varnot`'

`!include file`
> Include the specified file.

`!locale value`
> Load the following definitions only of the locale is set to *value*.

`!message text`
> Display *text* when the database is read unless the quiet option ('`-q`') is enabled.

`!set variable value`
> Sets the environment variable, *variable*, to the specified value *only if* it is not already set.

`!unitlist alias definition`
> Define a unit list alias.

`!utf8`   Load the following definitions only if **units** is running with UTF-8 enabled.

`!var envar value-list`
> Load the block of definitions that follows only if the environment variable *envar* is set to one of the values listed in the space-separated value list. If *envar* is not set, **units** prints an error message and ignores the block of definitions.

`!varnot envar value-list`
> Load the block of definitions that follows only if the environment variable *envar* is set to value that is *not* listed in the space-separated value list. If *envar* is not set, **units** prints an error message and ignores the block of definitions.

19 GNU Free Documentation License

Version 1.3, 3 November 2008

Copyright © 2000, 2001, 2002, 2007, 2008 Free Software Foundation, Inc.
`http://fsf.org/`

Everyone is permitted to copy and distribute verbatim copies
of this license document, but changing it is not allowed.

0. PREAMBLE

The purpose of this License is to make a manual, textbook, or other functional and useful document *free* in the sense of freedom: to assure everyone the effective freedom to copy and redistribute it, with or without modifying it, either commercially or non-commercially. Secondarily, this License preserves for the author and publisher a way to get credit for their work, while not being considered responsible for modifications made by others.

This License is a kind of "copyleft", which means that derivative works of the document must themselves be free in the same sense. It complements the GNU General Public License, which is a copyleft license designed for free software.

We have designed this License in order to use it for manuals for free software, because free software needs free documentation: a free program should come with manuals providing the same freedoms that the software does. But this License is not limited to software manuals; it can be used for any textual work, regardless of subject matter or whether it is published as a printed book. We recommend this License principally for works whose purpose is instruction or reference.

1. APPLICABILITY AND DEFINITIONS

This License applies to any manual or other work, in any medium, that contains a notice placed by the copyright holder saying it can be distributed under the terms of this License. Such a notice grants a world-wide, royalty-free license, unlimited in duration, to use that work under the conditions stated herein. The "Document", below, refers to any such manual or work. Any member of the public is a licensee, and is addressed as "you" You accept the license if you copy, modify or distribute the work in a way requiring permission under copyright law.

A "Modified Version' of the Document means any work containing the Document or a portion of it, either copied verbatim, or with modifications and/or translated into another language.

A "Secondary Section" is a named appendix or a front-matter section of the Document that deals exclusively with the relationship of the publishers or authors of the Document to the Document's overall subject (or to related matters) and contains nothing that could fall directly within that overall subject. (Thus, if the Document is in part a textbook of mathematics, a Secondary Section may not explain any mathematics.) The relationship could be a matter of historical connection with the subject or with related matters, or of legal, commercial, philosophical, ethical or political position regarding them.

The "Invariant Sections" are certain Secondary Sections whose titles are designated as being those of Invariant Sections, in the notice that says that the Document is released under this License. If a section does not fit the above definition of Secondary then it is not allowed to be designated as Invariant. The Document may contain zero Invariant Sections. If the Document does not identify any Invariant Sections then there are none.

The "Cover Texts" are certain short passages of text that are listed, as Front-Cover Texts or Back-Cover Texts, in the notice that says that the Document is released under this License. A Front-Cover Text may be at most 5 words, and a Back-Cover Text may be at most 25 words.

A "Transparent" copy of the Document means a machine-readable copy, represented in a format whose specification is available to the general public, that is suitable for revising the document straightforwardly with generic text editors or (for images composed of pixels) generic paint programs or (for drawings) some widely available drawing editor, and that is suitable for input to text formatters or for automatic translation to a variety of formats suitable for input to text formatters. A copy made in an otherwise Transparent file format whose markup, or absence of markup, has been arranged to thwart or discourage subsequent modification by readers is not Transparent. An image format is not Transparent if used for any substantial amount of text. A copy that is not "Transparent" is called "Opaque".

Examples of suitable formats for Transparent copies include plain ASCII without markup, Texinfo input format, LaTeX input format, SGML or XML using a publicly available DTD, and standard-conforming simple HTML, PostScript or PDF designed for human modification. Examples of transparent image formats include PNG, XCF and JPG. Opaque formats include proprietary formats that can be read and edited only by proprietary word processors, SGML or XML for which the DTD and/or processing tools are not generally available, and the machine-generated HTML, PostScript or PDF produced by some word processors for output purposes only.

The "Title Page" means, for a printed book, the title page itself, plus such following pages as are needed to hold, legibly, the material this License requires to appear in the title page. For works in formats which do not have any title page as such, "Title Page" means the text near the most prominent appearance of the work's title, preceding the beginning of the body of the text.

The "publisher" means any person or entity that distributes copies of the Document to the public.

A section "Entitled XYZ" means a named subunit of the Document whose title either is precisely XYZ or contains XYZ in parentheses following text that translates XYZ in another language. (Here XYZ stands for a specific section name mentioned below, such as "Acknowledgements", "Dedications", "Endorsements", or "History".) To "Preserve the Title" of such a section when you modify the Document means that it remains a section "Entitled XYZ" according to this definition.

The Document may include Warranty Disclaimers next to the notice which states that this License applies to the Document. These Warranty Disclaimers are considered to be included by reference in this License, but only as regards disclaiming warranties: any other implication that these Warranty Disclaimers may have is void and has no effect on the meaning of this License.

2. VERBATIM COPYING

You may copy and distribute the Document in any medium, either commercially or noncommercially, provided that this License, the copyright notices, and the license notice saying this License applies to the Document are reproduced in all copies, and that you add no other conditions whatsoever to those of this License. You may not use technical measures to obstruct or control the reading or further copying of the copies you make or distribute. However, you may accept compensation in exchange for copies. If you distribute a large enough number of copies you must also follow the conditions in section 3.

You may also lend copies, under the same conditions stated above, and you may publicly display copies.

3. COPYING IN QUANTITY

If you publish printed copies (or copies in media that commonly have printed covers) of the Document, numbering more than 100, and the Document's license notice requires Cover Texts, you must enclose the copies in covers that carry, clearly and legibly, all these Cover Texts: Front-Cover Texts on the front cover, and Back-Cover Texts on the back cover. Both covers must also clearly and legibly identify you as the publisher of these copies. The front cover must present the full title with all words of the title equally prominent and visible. You may add other material on the covers in addition. Copying with changes limited to the covers, as long as they preserve the title of the Document and satisfy these conditions, can be treated as verbatim copying in other respects.

If the required texts for either cover are too voluminous to fit legibly, you should put the first ones listed (as many as fit reasonably) on the actual cover, and continue the rest onto adjacent pages.

If you publish or distribute Opaque copies of the Document numbering more than 100, you must either include a machine-readable Transparent copy along with each Opaque copy, or state in or with each Opaque copy a computer-network location from which the general network-using public has access to download using public-standard network protocols a complete Transparent copy of the Document, free of added material. If you use the latter option, you must take reasonably prudent steps, when you begin distribution of Opaque copies in quantity, to ensure that this Transparent copy will remain thus accessible at the stated location until at least one year after the last time you distribute an Opaque copy (directly or through your agents or retailers) of that edition to the public.

It is requested, but not required, that you contact the authors of the Document well before redistributing any large number of copies, to give them a chance to provide you with an updated version of the Document.

4. MODIFICATIONS

You may copy and distribute a Modified Version of the Document under the conditions of sections 2 and 3 above, provided that you release the Modified Version under precisely this License, with the Modified Version filling the role of the Document, thus licensing distribution and modification of the Modified Version to whoever possesses a copy of it. In addition, you must do these things in the Modified Version:

A. Use in the Title Page (and on the covers, if any) a title distinct from that of the Document, and from those of previous versions (which should, if there were any, be listed in the History section of the Document). You may use the same title as a previous version if the original publisher of that version gives permission.

B. List on the Title Page, as authors, one or more persons or entities responsible for authorship of the modifications in the Modified Version, together with at least five of the principal authors of the Document (all of its principal authors, if it has fewer than five), unless they release you from this requirement.

C. State on the Title page the name of the publisher of the Modified Version, as the publisher.

D. Preserve all the copyright notices of the Document.

E. Add an appropriate copyright notice for your modifications adjacent to the other copyright notices.

F. Include, immediately after the copyright notices, a license notice giving the public permission to use the Modified Version under the terms of this License, in the form shown in the Addendum below.

G. Preserve in that license notice the full lists of Invariant Sections and required Cover Texts given in the Document's license notice.

H. Include an unaltered copy of this License.

I. Preserve the section Entitled "History", Preserve its Title, and add to it an item stating at least the title, year, new authors, and publisher of the Modified Version as given on the Title Page. If there is no section Entitled "History" in the Document, create one stating the title, year, authors, and publisher of the Document as given on its Title Page, then add an item describing the Modified Version as stated in the previous sentence.

J. Preserve the network location, if any, given in the Document for public access to a Transparent copy of the Document, and likewise the network locations given in the Document for previous versions it was based on. These may be placed in the "History" section. You may omit a network location for a work that was published at least four years before the Document itself, or if the original publisher of the version it refers to gives permission.

K. For any section Entitled "Acknowledgements" or "Dedications", Preserve the Title of the section, and preserve in the section all the substance and tone of each of the contributor acknowledgements and/or dedications given therein.

L. Preserve all the Invariant Sections of the Document, unaltered in their text and in their titles. Section numbers or the equivalent are not considered part of the section titles.

M. Delete any section Entitled "Endorsements". Such a section may not be included in the Modified Version.

N. Do not retitle any existing section to be Entitled "Endorsements" or to conflict in title with any Invariant Section.

O. Preserve any Warranty Disclaimers.

If the Modified Version includes new front-matter sections or appendices that qualify as Secondary Sections and contain no material copied from the Document, you may at your option designate some or all of these sections as invariant. To do this, add their titles to the list of Invariant Sections in the Modified Version's license notice. These titles must be distinct from any other section titles.

You may add a section Entitled "Endorsements", provided it contains nothing but endorsements of your Modified Version by various parties—for example, statements of peer review or that the text has been approved by an organization as the authoritative definition of a standard.

You may add a passage of up to five words as a Front-Cover Text, and a passage of up to 25 words as a Back-Cover Text, to the end of the list of Cover Texts in the Modified Version. Only one passage of Front-Cover Text and one of Back-Cover Text may be added by (or through arrangements made by) any one entity. If the Document already includes a cover text for the same cover, previously added by you or by arrangement made by the same entity you are acting on behalf of, you may not add another; but you may replace the old one, on explicit permission from the previous publisher that added the old one.

The author(s) and publisher(s) of the Document do not by this License give permission to use their names for publicity for or to assert or imply endorsement of any Modified Version.

5. COMBINING DOCUMENTS

You may combine the Document with other documents released under this License, under the terms defined in section 4 above for modified versions, provided that you include in the combination all of the Invariant Sections of all of the original documents, unmodified, and list them all as Invariant Sections of your combined work in its license notice, and that you preserve all their Warranty Disclaimers.

The combined work need only contain one copy of this License, and multiple identical Invariant Sections may be replaced with a single copy. If there are multiple Invariant Sections with the same name but different contents, make the title of each such section unique by adding at the end of it, in parentheses, the name of the original author or publisher of that section if known, or else a unique number. Make the same adjustment to the section titles in the list of Invariant Sections in the license notice of the combined work.

In the combination, you must combine any sections Entitled "History" in the various original documents, forming one section Entitled "History"; likewise combine any sections Entitled "Acknowledgements", and any sections Entitled "Dedications". You must delete all sections Entitled "Endorsements."

6. COLLECTIONS OF DOCUMENTS

You may make a collection consisting of the Document and other documents released under this License, and replace the individual copies of this License in the various documents with a single copy that is included in the collection, provided that you follow the rules of this License for verbatim copying of each of the documents in all other respects.

You may extract a single document from such a collection, and distribute it individually under this License, provided you insert a copy of this License into the extracted document, and follow this License in all other respects regarding verbatim copying of that document.

7. AGGREGATION WITH INDEPENDENT WORKS

A compilation of the Document or its derivatives with other separate and independent documents or works, in or on a volume of a storage or distribution medium, is called an "aggregate" if the copyright resulting from the compilation is not used to limit the legal rights of the compilation's users beyond what the individual works permit. When the Document is included in an aggregate, this License does not apply to the other works in the aggregate which are not themselves derivative works of the Document.

If the Cover Text requirement of section 3 is applicable to these copies of the Document, then if the Document is less than one half of the entire aggregate, the Document's Cover Texts may be placed on covers that bracket the Document within the aggregate, or the electronic equivalent of covers if the Document is in electronic form. Otherwise they must appear on printed covers that bracket the whole aggregate.

8. TRANSLATION

Translation is considered a kind of modification, so you may distribute translations of the Document under the terms of section 4. Replacing Invariant Sections with translations requires special permission from their copyright holders, but you may include translations of some or all Invariant Sections in addition to the original versions of these Invariant Sections. You may include a translation of this License, and all the license notices in the Document, and any Warranty Disclaimers, provided that you also include the original English version of this License and the original versions of those notices and disclaimers. In case of a disagreement between the translation and the original version of this License or a notice or disclaimer, the original version will prevail.

If a section in the Document is Entitled "Acknowledgements", "Dedications", or "History", the requirement (section 4) to Preserve its Title (section 1) will typically require changing the actual title.

9. TERMINATION

You may not copy, modify, sublicense, or distribute the Document except as expressly provided under this License. Any attempt otherwise to copy, modify, sublicense, or distribute it is void, and will automatically terminate your rights under this License.

However, if you cease all violation of this License, then your license from a particular copyright holder is reinstated (a) provisionally, unless and until the copyright holder explicitly and finally terminates your license, and (b) permanently, if the copyright holder fails to notify you of the violation by some reasonable means prior to 60 days after the cessation.

Moreover, your license from a particular copyright holder is reinstated permanently if the copyright holder notifies you of the violation by some reasonable means, this is the first time you have received notice of violation of this License (for any work) from that copyright holder, and you cure the violation prior to 30 days after your receipt of the notice.

Termination of your rights under this section does not terminate the licenses of parties who have received copies or rights from you under this License. If your rights have been terminated and not permanently reinstated, receipt of a copy of some or all of the same material does not give you any rights to use it.

10. FUTURE REVISIONS OF THIS LICENSE

The Free Software Foundation may publish new, revised versions of the GNU Free Documentation License from time to time. Such new versions will be similar in spirit to the present version, but may differ in detail to address new problems or concerns. See http://www.gnu.org/copyleft/.

Each version of the License is given a distinguishing version number. If the Document specifies that a particular numbered version of this License "or any later version" applies to it, you have the option of following the terms and conditions either of that specified version or of any later version that has been published (not as a draft) by the Free Software Foundation. If the Document does not specify a version number of this License, you may choose any version ever published (not as a draft) by the Free

Software Foundation. If the Document specifies that a proxy can decide which future versions of this License can be used, that proxy's public statement of acceptance of a version permanently authorizes you to choose that version for the Document.

11. RELICENSING

"Massive Multiauthor Collaboration Site" (or "MMC Site") means any World Wide Web server that publishes copyrightable works and also provides prominent facilities for anybody to edit those works. A public wiki that anybody can edit is an example of such a server. A "Massive Multiauthor Collaboration" (or "MMC") contained in the site means any set of copyrightable works thus published on the MMC site.

"CC-BY-SA" means the Creative Commons Attribution-Share Alike 3.0 license published by Creative Commons Corporation, a not-for-profit corporation with a principal place of business in San Francisco, California, as well as future copyleft versions of that license published by that same organization.

"Incorporate" means to publish or republish a Document, in whole or in part, as part of another Document.

An MMC is "eligible for relicensing" if it is licensed under this License, and if all works that were first published under this License somewhere other than this MMC, and subsequently incorporated in whole or in part into the MMC, (1) had no cover texts or invariant sections, and (2) were thus incorporated prior to November 1, 2008.

The operator of an MMC Site may republish an MMC contained in the site under CC-BY-SA on the same site at any time before August 1, 2009, provided the MMC is eligible for relicensing.

ADDENDUM: How to use this License for your documents

To use this License in a document you have written, include a copy of the License in the document and put the following copyright and license notices just after the title page:

```
Copyright (C)  year   your name.
Permission is granted to copy, distribute and/or modify this document
under the terms of the GNU Free Documentation License, Version 1.3
or any later version published by the Free Software Foundation;
with no Invariant Sections, no Front-Cover Texts, and no Back-Cover
Texts.  A copy of the license is included in the section entitled ''GNU
Free Documentation License''.
```

If you have Invariant Sections, Front-Cover Texts and Back-Cover Texts, replace the "with. . . Texts." line with this:

```
with the Invariant Sections being list their titles, with
the Front-Cover Texts being list, and with the Back-Cover Texts
being list.
```

If you have Invariant Sections without Cover Texts, or some other combination of the three, merge those two alternatives to suit the situation.

If your document contains nontrivial examples of program code, we recommend releasing these examples in parallel under your choice of free software license, such as the GNU General Public License, to permit their use in free software.

Index

www.ingramcontent.com/pod-product-compliance
Lightning Source LLC
Chambersburg PA
CBHW060005230526
45472CB00008B/1955

*9 7 8 9 8 8 8 3 8 1 5 2 4 *